SHORT WALKS IN NIDDERDALE

by Jon Fallis

Looking along Nidderdale to Gouthwaite Reservoir

CONTENTS

USING THIS GUIDE

Routes in this book

In this book you will find a selection of easy or moderate walks suitable for almost everyone, including casual walkers and families with children, or for when you only have a short time to fill. The routes have been carefully chosen to allow you to explore the area and its attractions. Although there may be some climbs there is no challenging terrain, but do bear in mind that conditions can sometimes be wet or muddy underfoot. A route summary table is included on page 6 to help you choose the right walk.

Clothing and footwear

You won't need any special equipment to enjoy these walks. The weather in Britain can be changeable, so choose clothing suitable for the season and wear or carry a waterproof jacket. For footwear, comfortable walking boots or trainers with a good grip are best. A small rucksack for drinks, snacks and spare clothing is useful. See www.adventuresmart.uk.

Walk descriptions

At the beginning of each walk you'll find all the information you need:

- start/finish location, with postcode and a what3words address to help you find it
- parking and transport information, estimated walking time, total distance and climb
- details of public toilets available along the route and where you can get refreshments
- a summary of the key highlights of the walk and what you might see

Timings given are the time to complete the walk at a reasonable walking pace. Allow extra time for extended stops or if walking with children.

The route is described in clear, easy-to-follow directions, with each waypoint marked on an accompanying map extract. It's a good idea to read the whole of the route instructions before setting out, so that you know what to expect.

Maps, GPX files and what3words

Extracts from the OS 1:25,000 map accompany each route. GPX files for all the walks in this book are available to download at www.cicerone.co.uk/1154/gpx.

What3words is a free smartphone app which identifies every 3m square of the globe with a unique three-word address, e.g. ///destiny.cafe.sonic. For more information see https://what3words.com/products/what3words-app.

Walking with children

Even young children can be surprisingly strong walkers, but every family is different and you may need to adapt the timings given in this book to take that into account. Make sure you go at the pace of the slowest member and choose a walk with an exciting objective in mind, such as a cave, waterfall or picnic spot. Many of the walks can be shortened to suit – suggestions are included at the end of the route description.

Dogs

Sheep or cattle may be found grazing on a number of these walks. Keep dogs under control at all times so that they don't scare or disturb livestock or wildlife. Cattle, particularly cows with calves, may very occasionally pose a risk to walkers with dogs. If you ever feel threatened by cattle, you should let go of your dog's lead and let it run free.

Enjoying the countryside responsibly

Enjoy the countryside and treat it with respect to protect our natural environments. Stick to footpaths and take your litter home with you. When driving, slow down on rural roads and park considerately, or better still use public transport. For more details check out www.gov.uk/countryside-code.

The Countryside Code

Respect everyone

- be considerate to those living in, working in and enjoying the countryside
- leave gates and property as you find them
- do not block access to gateways or driveways when parking
- be nice, say hello, share the space
- follow local signs and keep to marked paths unless wider access is available

Protect the environment

- take your litter home – leave no trace of your visit
- do not light fires and only have BBQs where signs say you can
- always keep dogs under control and in sight
- dog poo – bag it and bin it – any public waste bin will do
- care for nature – do not cause damage or disturbance

Enjoy the outdoors

- check your route and local conditions
- plan your adventure – know what to expect and what you can do
- enjoy your visit, have fun, make a memory

ROUTE SUMMARY TABLE

WALK NAME	START POINT	TIME	DISTANCE
1. Jervaulx Abbey	Jervaulx Abbey	3hr 20min	11.5km (7¼ miles)
2. Colsterdale heritage walk	Gollinglith Foot	1hr 45min	5.5km (3½ miles)
3. Masham river walk	Masham	1hr 30min	5.5km (3½ miles)
4. Hackfall and Grewelthorpe	Hackfall near Grewelthorpe	1hr 30min	4.5km (2¾ miles)
5. Dallowgill	Tom Corner near Dallowgill	1hr 30 min	4.5km (2¾ miles)
6. How Stean Gorge	Middlesmoor	1hr	3km (1¾ miles)
7. Pateley Bridge river walk	Pateley Bridge	1hr 30min	5km (3 miles)
8. Coldstones Cut	Greenhow	30min	1.5km (1 mile)
9. Brimham Rocks	Brimham Rocks	1hr 20min	4km (2½ miles)
10. Studley Royal	Studley Royal	2hr	6.5km (4 miles)
11. Dacre Banks riverside walk	Dacre Banks	1hr 45min	6.5km (4 miles)
12. Ripley circular	Ripley	1hr 15min	4.5km (2¾ miles)
13. Nidd Gorge	Knaresborough	2hr 30min	9km (5½ miles)
14. Swinsty Reservoir	Swinsty and Fewston Reservoir	1hr 30min	5km (3 miles)
15. Washburn valley circular	Lindley Reservoir	3hr	9.5km (6 miles)

HIGHLIGHTS

Abbey ruins, river and peaceful scenery

Remote dale with industrial and military history

Historic town, two rivers and artwork

Woodland garden with follies and grottos

Moorland and woods, great views and mosaics

Steep gorge and spectacular upland scenery

Pretty town, art, architecture and history

Contemporary artwork, industry and far-ranging views

Spectacular rock formations, moors, woods and farmland

Beautiful gardens, parkland and secluded valley

Farmland, river and two pretty villages

Picturesque village, castle and views

Ancient woodland, lovely market town and river

Woodland, water and valley views

Woods, river and farmland with great views

SYMBOLS USED ON ROUTE MAPS

S Start point

F Finish point

SF Start and finish at the same place

Waypoint

Route line

MAPPING IS SHOWN AT A SCALE OF 1:25,000

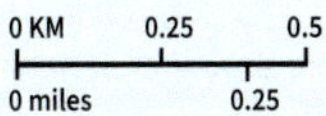

DOWNLOADED THE GPX FILES FOR FREE AT
www.cicerone.co.uk/1154/GPX

Dales barn and meadow

INTRODUCTION

Typical lower Nidderdale scenery

This guidebook is a collection of walks in and around the Nidderdale Area of Outstanding Natural Beauty (AONB) in North Yorkshire. Covering approximately 600 sq km, Nidderdale AONB covers the eastern portion of the Yorkshire Dales and stretches towards the Vale of York. Within its boundaries is a rich and varied landscape, from open heather moorlands and steep river valleys to woodlands and rolling pastures, and from drystone walls and traditional field barns to lovely towns and pretty villages.

At the heart of the AONB is the River Nidd, but it also incorporates other dales (Wensleydale and Colsterdale) and related rivers. The River Ure carves a route around the north and east of the area and is fed by the rivers Burn, Laver and Skell. The Washburn valley, which makes up the southern portion of the Nidderdale AONB, feeds into Wharfdale and is now dominated by four reservoirs. The AONB is a rich area for wildlife, as the diverse habitats, from moorlands to rare hay meadows in the valley bottoms, support a great variety of wildlife and plants. This diversity of landscape and wildlife means it is home to nine Sites of Special Scientific Interest (SSSI), many of which feature on walks in this book. This fascinating landscape of contrasts has been shaped by its geology, with gritstone overlaying limestone. Over the centuries humans have found different ways to exploit the area's resources, whether through farming, mining, quarrying, reservoirs or, increasingly, tourism. Historically this created wealth, which in turn has left a rich heritage, with significant buildings and designed landscapes of varying degrees of grandeur, like Fountains Abbey. These historic parks and gardens, along with some of the more spectacular landforms, such as Brimham Rocks, distinguish Nidderdale AONB from its more famous neighbour the Yorkshire Dales National Park.

Walking in Nidderdale

The 15 walks in this guide are designed to showcase the beauty of this wonderful part of the world. The walks are broadly divided into three areas: Lower Swaledale, Nidderdale and the Washburn valley that feeds the River Wharf.

The routes have been chosen to reflect the varied nature of the area. There are routes which explore historic buildings, parks and gardens such as Studley Royal (Walk 10), Jervaulx Abbey (Walk 1) and Hackfall (Walk 4). Others focus on the landscape, including Brimham Rocks (Walk 9), Nidd Gorge (Walk 13) and How Stean Gorge (Walk 6), or on the man-made reservoirs that form an important haven for wildlife (Walks 14 and 15). Routes are in general well-signposted and on good paths, though some can be muddy.

Pateley Bridge high street

AONB boundary sign

Bases

The only town within the AONB boundary is Pateley Bridge, which is the physical and spiritual heart of Nidderdale and marks the boundary between the upper and lower Nidd. Further afield Masham, Ripon, Harrogate, Knaresborough, Ilkely and Otley are well served by public transport, with accommodation, cafes, restaurants and pubs, and all make good bases for exploring the area covered by the book.

Travel

The Nidderdale AONB is entirely rural and this means the easiest way to access the walks is by car. Many of the roads are minor roads, so allow plenty of time to get around. The only A-roads are the A59, which bisects the area in the southern quarter, and the A61, which runs near the eastern boundary between Harrogate and Ripon. The area is served by some bus links (Dales Bus) which are regular, if not frequent. Only one walk (Walk 13 Nidd Gorge) can be accessed by train. Where possible the walks are located so they offer some form of public transport and/or free parking (at time of writing).

The entire western edge of Nidderdale AONB borders the Yorkshire Dales National Park so access is from the east and south. The key access points are Masham, Ripon, Harrogate/Knaresborough and Ilkley/Otley. The nearest train stations are Harrogate or Knaresborough, both with regular services from London, Leeds and York.

Medieval sundial
near Jervaulx Abbey

WALK 1

Jervaulx Abbey

Time 3hr 20min
Distance 11.5km (7¼ miles)
Climb 110m

A scenic walk through farmland, offering glimpses of ancient history in a lovely landscape

Start/finish	*Jervaulx Abbey*
Locate	*HG4 4PH ///bookings.formally.demanding*
Cafes/pubs	*Pub at Cover Bridge*
Transport	*Bus 825 to entrance to Jervaulx, from York or Richmond*
Parking	*Jervaulx Abbey car park (honesty box)*
Toilets	*No public toilets on route*

This gentle walk starts and finishes at the ruins of an 11th-century abbey. It incorporates a Norman bridge built over a Roman ford, a 9th-century church and a 15th-century manor house, Danby Hall. In between is gently rolling farmland and riverside paths along the River Ure in Swaledale. The walk is well signposted and mostly paved but some of it is across farmland so can be muddy at certain times of the year. Take time to walk around the abbey ruins at the start or end of the walk.

Looking towards Thornton Steward

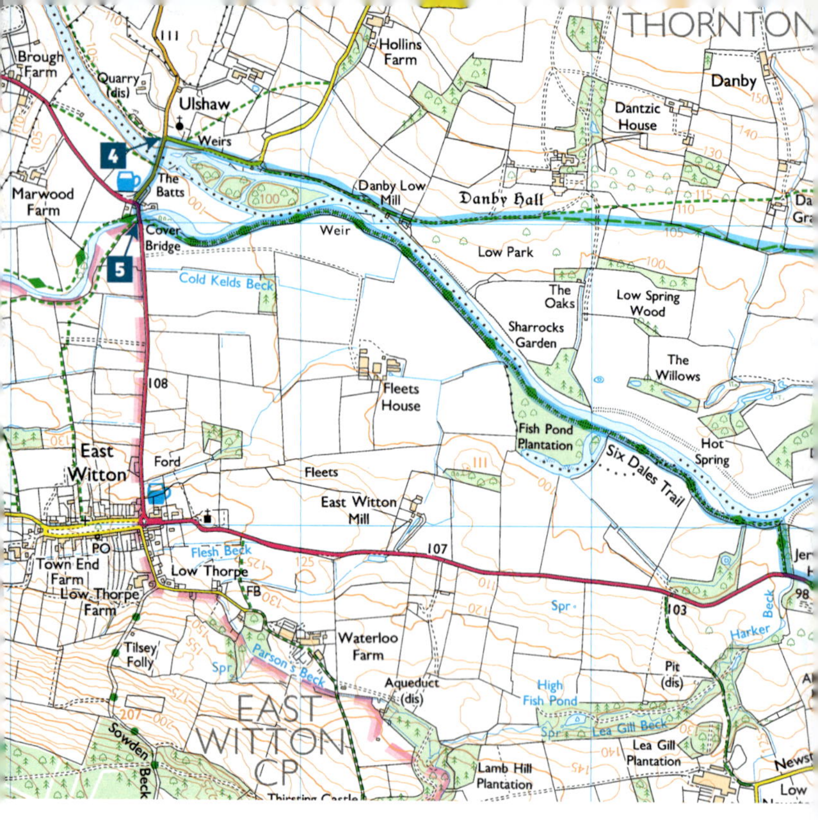

1 Start at the road entrance to the abbey car park. Cross the road and go through the iron gate into the grounds of **Jervaulx Abbey**. Follow the gravel path towards the abbey until you meet a tarmac track, then turn right to follow the track as it passes the abbey on the left. Continue along the track, passing a track junction then a pond, to reach an entrance gate and a road (**Kilgram Lane**). Turn left and follow the road to a bridge.

According to legend the bridge got its name because the Devil offered to keep the bridge safe from floods as long as a sacrifice was made. That sacrifice was a shepherd's dog called Grim and this has evolved into the name Kilgram Bridge.

2 Once across the bridge stop at the second set of double gates to the left, cross a stile and follow a track that

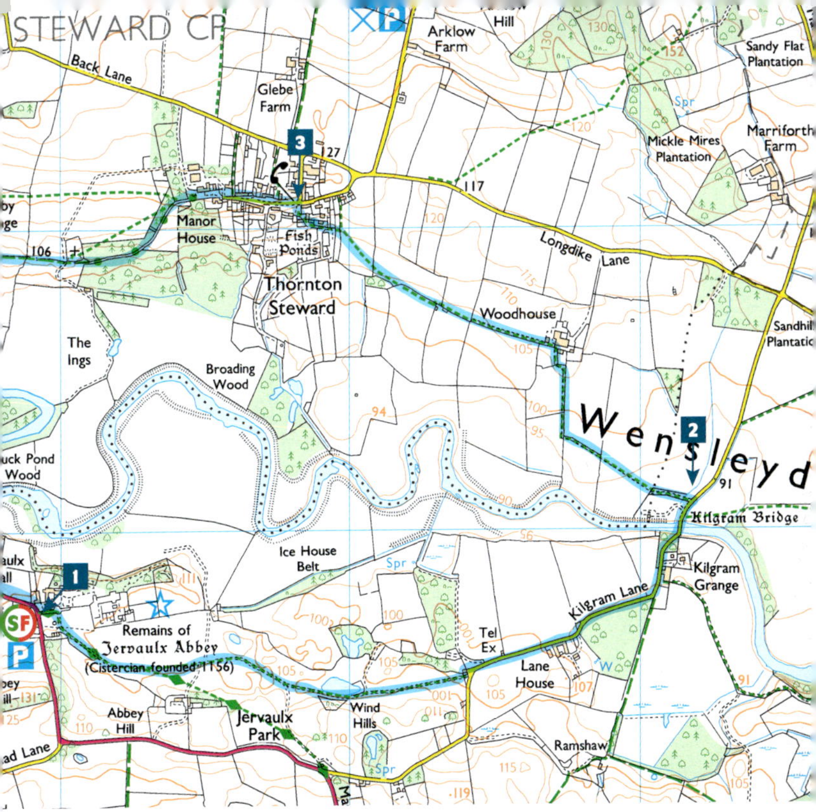

STEWARD CP

Hill

Arklow Farm

Sandy Flat Plantation

Back Lane

Glebe Farm

3

127

Marriforth Farm

Mickle Mires Plantation

117

Manor House

Fish Ponds

Longdike Lane

Thornton Steward

Woodhouse

The Ings

Broading Wood

Sandhill Plantatic

Wensleyd

2

uck Pond Wood

Kilgram Bridge

Ice House Belt

1

Kilgram Grange

Kilgram Lane

Remains of Jervaulx Abbey (Cistercian founded 1156)

Tel Ex

Lane House

Abbey Hill

Jervaulx Park

Wind Hills

Ramshaw

ad Lane

Kilgram Bridge

Danby Hall seen from the path

leads into a field. Cross the field, go through a gate, then over a stile and through another gate. On the other side of the hedge turn right to walk towards **Woodhouse** farm then go through a farm gate, off to the left. Cross the field to a metal barn, go through a gate and turn left in front of the barn to go through a further gate into a field. Continue through the fields towards a village ahead (note footpath signs and white posts). Go through a gap in a fence then a gate with a horse riding arena to the left. Follow signs to Carbridge and reach a road in **Thornton Steward**.

3 Turn left to pass a water pump and reach a brown wooden gate ahead with the Manor House to the left. Go through the gate and follow the track as it descends into woodland and then passes 9th-century St Oswald's Church. Follow the level path across fields and eventually in front of the impressive **Danby Hall**. The path gently descends to exit the estate onto a tarmac single-track road. When the path meets a wider road, turn left and follow it to a T-junction.

ⓘ *The River Nidd was given its name by the Celts, from the word for flowing or sparkling (depending on which source is believed).*

4 Turn left across the bridge then at the next T-junction turn left to cross **Cover Bridge**. This is a narrow humpback bridge, so care is needed if it is busy.

5 Immediately at the far end of the bridge go left down some steps to get off the road. Follow the path along the river until it reaches some wooden fencing which points the path to the right to reach the road. Turn left to follow the road back to the start.

– To shorten

For a riverside walk of about 5km (1hr 30min), from the start walk back towards Cover Bridge (Waypoint 5) and return. It is a level walk but can be muddy.

Jervaulx Abbey

Jervaulx Abbey

Built around 1158, Jervaulx was a daughter house to nearby Byland Abbey. A Cistercian monastery, it was ruined as part of the dissolution of the monasteries in the time of Henry VIII, and material from the ruins can be seen in churches in the surrounding area. As well as its beautiful location, Jervaulx is noted for the large number of wildflowers that grow amongst the abbey walls. Kilgram Bridge across the River Ure was built to supply the abbey. It was built on the site of a Roman ford, which is still visible below the bridge.

Leeds Pals memorial

WALK 2

Colsterdale heritage walk

Start/finish	*Gollinglith Foot*
Locate	*HG4 4LL ///handy.rings.delighted*
Cafes/pubs	*None on route*
Transport	*No public transport*
Parking	*Small car park at Gollinglith Foot (free)*
Toilets	*No public toilets on route*

Time 1hr 45min
Distance 5.5km (3½ miles)
Climb 160m

A circular walk around a remote dale that reveals its industrial and military history at every turn

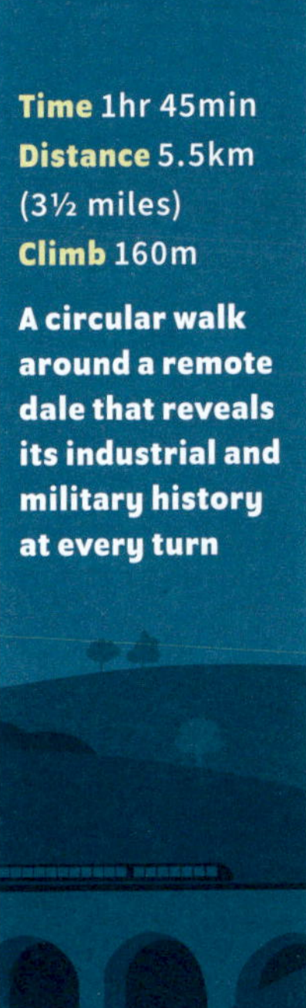

This walk along quiet roads and across farm fields reveals an incredible industrial and military history for such a remote dale. Between 1900 and 1930 this quiet dale hosted work, army training and prisoner-of-war camps, and there is evidence of this at every turn. The army training camp was for the 'Leeds Pals', formed early in WW1, and is remembered with a memorial visited on the walk. The route is well marked but is quite remote.

View across Colsterdale

Old railway bed near Leighton Bridge

1 From the phone box by the car park, walk back along the road as it gently ascends to offer great views around the area. Your destination, the Leeds Pals memorial cairn, can be seen across the valley.

2 At a junction turn right along the road, following the sign for 'Leeds pals memorial', and descend past a layby on the right just before a small bridge. In the field on your left you can see the bed of an old narrow-gauge railway. Cross **Leighton Bridge**.

3 Immediately after the bridge take the next right to follow the road uphill, passing a Methodist church, and continue on to arrive at the **war memorial** cairn. Carry on along the road to reach a pair of metal gates, one in front and one to your right.

4 Go through the gate to the right with a bridleway sign. Follow the tarmac track downhill towards a farm, **Spout House**. As the track bends left, follow footpath signs through a red farm gate to the right and then bend left to go round a building to a gate into a neighbouring field. Walk downhill through the field to a small wooden gate. Go through the gate and follow the path downhill to a footbridge over a water channel. Follow signs through a further gate into a field and slightly right, through some trees, to a further gate into woodland. Cross a small stream and then exit the woodland into a field. Cross the field, keeping the buildings to your left, and at a signpost go through a gap in a hedge, then bear slightly left across the field to a gap in the gorse. Go through the gap and descend to a farm gate. Turn right to cross the bridge and return to the start.

View of original gates to work camp

Unique signs on the Colsterdale walk

– To shorten

Park at the layby before Leighton Bridge (Waypoint 2) and walk up to the memorial cairn and back. Return distance approximately 2km (45min).

+ To lengthen

At Waypoint 3 continue along road for 1.5km to see Leighton Reservoir and views along the valley. This will add approximately 3km and 1hr to the total walk.

Leeds Pals memorial cairn

Take time to stop and read about the various camps located nearby between 1904 and the mid 1920s. This dale housed the workers who built Leighton Reservoir. Evidence of this can still be seen, such as the bed of the narrow-gauge railway at Waypoint 2. Early in WW1 the camp was used as a British Army training camp and later became a prisoner-of-war camp housing German officers. After the war it returned to its original purpose as a labour camp for reservoir building.

Looking across the final footbridge to the start/end point

Market cross in Masham town square

WALK 3

Masham river walk

Start/finish	*Riverside in Masham*
Locate	*HG4 4DS (cricket club) ///dormant.rocker.sensitive*
Cafes/pubs	*Cafes, pubs, hotels and two breweries in Masham*
Transport	*Buses 138 from Ripon, 144 from Bedale, 159 Ripon/Richmond, 825 from Richmond/Ripon*
Parking	*Riverside car park (with honesty box), first left after crossing Masham Bridge. Some off-street paid parking around town and limited free on-street parking*
Toilets	*Near the tourist office just off the town square*

Time 1hr 30min
Distance 5.5km (3½ miles)
Climb 30m

A gentle river walk from the cricket club to the town square along the rivers Ure and Burn, with some locally quarried artwork to see

A gentle walk around this lovely town takes in two rivers and some artwork. The town even has two famous breweries. Finish the walk with an amble around the Georgian town square, thought to be one of the largest in England. The walk is well signposted but can be muddy in places. The path is close to the river and where the river meanders, over time, this may move the path.

Looking across Masham cricket ground to the town beyond

Signpost in Masham market square

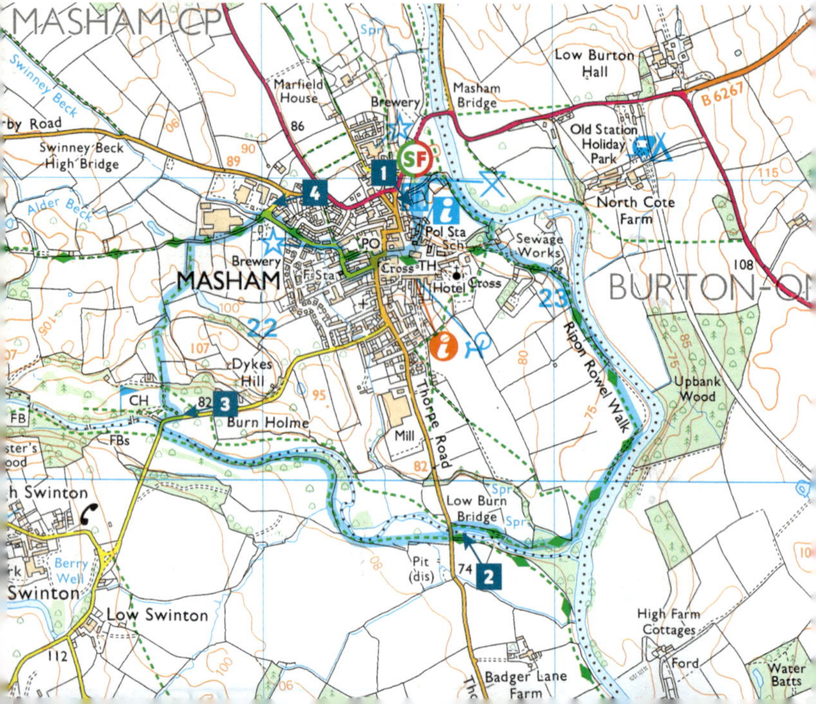

1 Start near the honesty box in the car park. Walk to the riverside path and turn right to skirt the cricket pitch. Pass a house, walk along its drive to reach a road, turn left and keep with the single-track road as it passes the water treatment works then follows the **River Ure** as it meanders right. Eventually the path enters a wood and reaches a road and **Low Burn Bridge**.

2 Turn left to cross the bridge, then turn immediately right to go through a metal gate. Follow the path, keeping the **River Burn** to your right. At a stile into a field go over the stile then cross back over another stile. The path descends to the river bank. Turn left to follow the river until you reach the golf course. Keep right and go through a metal gate, then cross a footbridge and skirt the golf course. Eventually a metal gate leads onto the course. Keep right and follow the path to the road.

ⓘ ***Masham market received its charter in 1251, which gave the town the right to hold two markets every week.***

View of the path through the trees

Turn right, cross the bridge and then turn left to go through the entrance to the golf club.

3 Just beyond the entrance, follow the track left across the fairway. At the far side turn right to follow footpath signs over a stile across a field, then go through two metal gates and a further gate, still following yellow footpath signs. Enter a field and walk towards a large building ahead. The path crosses the field to reach a track through a gate. Turn right along the track to pass in front of the building and cross a humpback bridge to a road junction.

Masham Leaves

Masham Leaves is a series of sculptures produced in the early 1990s by Alain Ayres from locally quarried limestone reclaimed from the former railway station platform. The walk described here crosses part of this longer route and takes in three leaves: Leaf 3 'Floating Leaf', Leaf 4 'Shrine' and Leaf 5 'Enclosure'. The full Masham Leaves route is approximately 5km. You can pick up a leaflet from the tourist office.

Masham Leaves sculpture no. 5 'Enclosure'

Masham town crest near market square

ⓘ *Masham can be considered the home of English beer, with two famous breweries (Theakstons & Black Sheep).*

4 At the junction turn right onto Westholme Road, then follow the road as it bends to the right and passes the Theakstons **brewery**. At a T-junction with Park Street, turn left to follow the road until it becomes Church Street. Pass an entrance to the town square and at a bend cross the road to Little Market Place. Walk to the far side of the tourist information office and turn left (signed 'public toilets') then go down steps to the cricket club and car park beyond.

View of the River Ure through Hackfall woods

WALK 4

Hackfall and Grewelthorpe

Start/finish	*Hackfall near Grewelthorpe*
Locate	*HG4 3BS ///foresight.airship.renders*
Cafes/pubs	*Pub in Grewelthorpe*
Transport	*Bus 159 (Ripon–Leyburn) stops at Hackfall*
Parking	*Woodland Trust car park (free) north of Grewelthorpe, on the Masham road*
Toilets	*No public toilets on route*

Thread your way through a maze of paths that reveal man-made and natural wonders at every turn. There are grottos, waterfalls, temples and wooded glades to explore, a detour to a pretty village and glimpses of some great views to the east. The route is well signposted but follows muddy paths, often with tree roots protruding. Some paths are steep or have steep drops off to the side and there is almost no access for wheelchairs or prams.

Time 1 hr 30min
Distance 4.5km (2¾ miles)
Climb 190m

A beautiful hillside that blends ancient woodland with man-made grottos, follies, temples and waterfalls to create a wooded wonderland

Fishers Hall folly

1 From the back of the car park follow the steps to a gate and once through turn left to follow the path downhill. After about 100m reach a farm gate, turn right and then go through a kissing gate. Follow the track as it crosses a field to another gate and enter the wood. The path runs along the top of a steep slope, then skirts a building, passes a stone structure (the Ruin) and gently descends to a sharp bend.

The story of Hackfall goes back to at least the 11th century. The Domesday Book records that before the Norman Conquest the area was held by a Saxon lord named Gospatric, the Earl of Dunbar.

2 At the path bend follow signs for Grewelthorpe, cross a bridge and exit the woods into a field. At a Y-junction in the field follow the path to the right to go through a hedge and join a track. Turn right to follow the track to meet the road through the pretty village of **Grewelthorpe**. At the road turn right and follow it around a sharp bend (no footway), then turn right to follow a footpath into the woods and back to the bend at Waypoint 2.

Alum Spring in Hackfall

3 Now follow signs to 'Fountain pond & follies' then turn right to follow signs to 'Alum Springs'. The springs yield tufa, a soft porous rock that is deposited by a chemical process from this calcite-rich water. After Alum Spring continue to follow the path downhill, keeping a stream to your left. This leads to a track junction with a post signed 'Ripon Rowel'. Take

ⓘ Hackfall is a designated Site of Special Scientific Interest (SSSI) because of the large number of birds, plants and invertebrates that live or feed here.

the right path that leads to the 'Fishers Hall' folly. Follow the path and steps on the far side of Fishers Hall to reach the **River Ure**.

4 At the river turn left to follow an undulating, muddy riverside path. This meets a wider gravel path – at this point follow the orange arrow and the path passes two stone pillars.

5 After the pillars turn left and follow signs uphill to the car park to return to the start.

– To shorten

At Waypoint 2 turn left to miss out Grewelthorpe, saving around 40min.

+ To lengthen

The route described here covers a fraction of the woods. Continue to explore other path options (site maps are usually available at the car park).

Hackfall

Boundary sign at Hackfall

A beautiful Grade 1 listed woodland garden with follies, waterfalls and surprise views, Hackfall was created in the 18th century by William Aislabie, owner of Studley Royal and Fountains Abbey. The woodland covers 47 hectares (120 acres) of ancient semi-natural woodland rising above the steep gorge of the River Ure. As well as being a haven for wildlife and a designated Site of Special Scientific Interest, it has won a European Union heritage prize for conservation of the landscape.

WALK 5

Dallowgill

Start/finish	*On the moor above Tom Corner near Dallowgill*
Locate	*HG4 3QY (houses at Tom Corner) ///ties.ditching.loafer*
Cafes/pubs	*None on route*
Transport	*No public transport*
Parking	*Small car park at Tom Corner courtesy of the Dallowgill Estate*
Toilets	*No public toilets on route*

Time 1hr 30min
Distance 4.5km (2¾ miles)
Climb 110m

A peaceful walk through an upland area offering great views, with some ceramic artwork adding extra interest

This is a walk of two halves. The first half follows a road from open moorland into the wooded valley below, the second goes through woods and across farmland to return to the start. Views to the south and east can be amazing and the route incorporates a Victorian monument and some artwork, part of what is known as the Crackpots Mosaic Trail.

View across Dallowgill from Greygarth Monument

Views towards Fountains Abbey and Ripon

Roman soldier mosaic

1 From the car park walk downhill along the road back to the road junction. At the junction turn right to follow signs to Dallowgill. Continue along the road as it gently descends, cross a cattle-grid and then reach a junction with a road off to the left. Cross a ladder stile and ascend through the field to reach the rectangular **Greygarth Monument**.

Greygarth Monument was a ruin until it was rebuilt in 1984. The plaque states that the tower was created for Queen Victoria's jubilee in 1897 but there is evidence that something has stood on this spot since 1838.

2 Retrace your steps back down across the ladder stile and continue along the road as it descends, passing

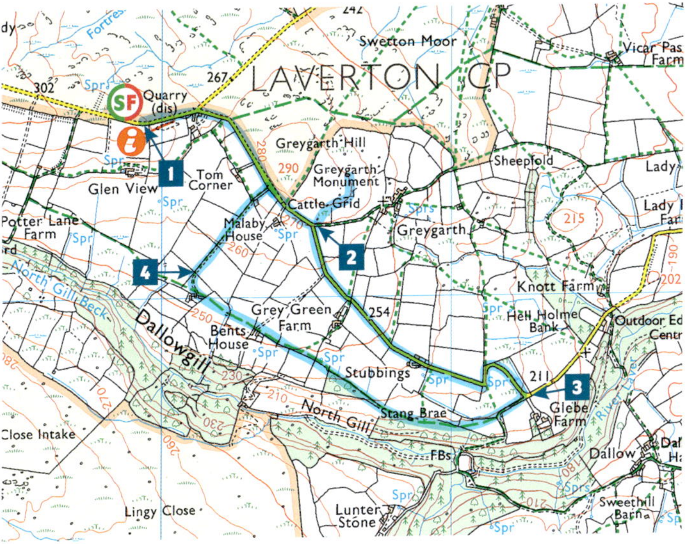

Looking across Dallowgill to the heather moorland beyond

Grey Green Farm and then **Stubbings Farm**. After a further few hundred metres of descent the road meanders left then right then after a further 100m the road turns sharp left opposite a house (the Old Vicarage).

3 At this point turn right onto a gravel track signposted as a bridleway and continue to where it bends left to descend into woodland. Go through a farm gate to the right, signed 'Bridleway', into a field and aim for the far-left hand corner. Go through a further wooden gate into woods. Note the mosaic on far side of the gate. Continue along the path to reach a small wooden gate into a field, cross the field and go through two further gates across two more fields. The final gate leads in front of **Bents House**. Walk past the house then go through a metal gate at the far corner of the house (note a ceramic yellow footpath

Ceramic waymark

Dallowgill takes its name from Dallow, the small group of houses to the south of this walk. It is derived from 'dael haga', meaning enclosure in the dale.

sign on the wall of the house). Cross a further field, aiming towards buildings, go through a wooden gate and in the field in front of the building aim for the far right-hand corner.

4 Go through a metal farm gate in the corner, then follow footpath signs through gates/fields to reach the road. Turn left and simply retrace your steps to the start.

– To shorten

Walk to the Greygarth Monument then retrace your steps to the start, approximately 2km there and back.

Crackpots Mosaic Trail

The Crackpots Mosaic Trail was created in 1997 as part of a community project to celebrate the designation of Nidderdale as an AONB. Along the trail 22 ceramic mosaics depict local scenes. The full trail is 11km long, but on the walk described here you can find five of the mosaics: Mosaic 1 'Sheep' and Mosaic 22 'Roman Soldier' (in Waypoint 1); Mosaic 18 'Rabbits', Mosaic 19 'Barn Owl' and Mosaic 20 'Bents House' (in Waypoint 3). For the full trail see https://nidderdaleaonb.org.uk/wp-content/uploads/2020/12/Crackpots-Mosaic-Walking-Trail-Nidderdale-AONB.pdf

One of the Crackpots mosaics

View towards Middlesmoor church

WALK 6

How Stean Gorge

Start/finish	*Middlesmoor*
Locate	*HG3 5ST (hotel) ///talent.astounded.wheels*
Cafes/pubs	*Hotel by car park and cafe at How Stean Gorge*
Transport	*Bus 821 to Lofthouse (1km from start)*
Parking	*Public car park at the top of Middlesmoor (free)*
Toilets	*In Middlesmoor by the hotel*

Starting from one of the highest and most isolated villages in North Yorkshire, this circuit descends from Middlesmoor to walk around an amazing limestone gorge then returns through farmland. On the way there are great views along Nidderdale. This route can be muddy and there may be cattle in some of the fields. While the walk provides good views of How Stean Gorge, for a close-up view of the gorge and cave system you need to pay an entrance fee.

Looking along upper Nidderdale from the road below Middlesmoor

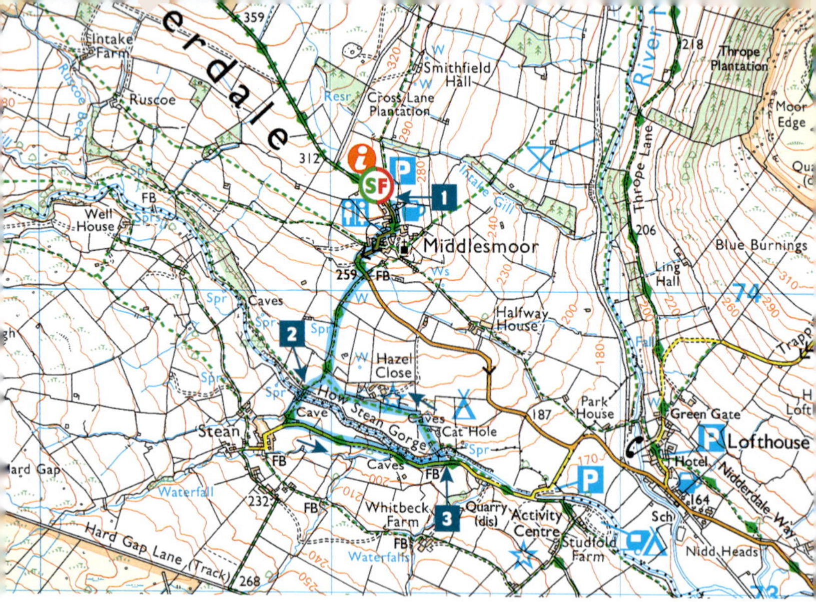

1 Turn left out of the car park to walk back through **Middlesmoor**. Follow the road as it leaves the village then starts to bend left. Opposite an old barn turn right, signed 'Nidderdale Way', go through the gap in the stone wall and descend through the field. After crossing two more walls look out for a stile in the wall to the right. Go through and descend diagonally right to the woods.

2 Go through the gate into the woods and down to a narrow foot-bridge, following signs for Nidderdale Way/Stean). Cross the bridge (the gorge is visible at this point) and follow the path as it ascends past a

Entrance to How Stean Gorge visitor centre

static caravan to reach a single-track road. Turn left and follow the road to the entrance to **How Stean Gorge**. Glimpses of the gorge can be seen from the road.

Highwayman Tom Taylor terrorised isolated villages and travellers in upper Nidderdale during the 18th century. He often hid in the caves in How Stean Gorge. He was eventually tracked by soldiers to one cave network and there met his end.

3 Turn left into the gorge complex, pass the cafe and cross the bridge. Walk to the back of the car park, pass the wooden lodges and go through the gap in the drystone wall beyond into a field. Follow red paint and yellow way-marker posts diagonally left through the field to a farm gate and across two more fields to a third gate. Once through this third gate aim for the top right of the field, still following markers, to rejoin your outbound route. Retrace your steps uphill to return to Middlesmoor and the start point.

How Stean Gorge

Looking down into the limestone gorge

How Stean Gorge was created when glacial and river water gouged huge gaps in the relatively soft limestone. The area has been designated a SSSI due to its unique landscape of gorges and caves. How Stean Gorge is approximately 1km in length and up to 26m deep. Because of its steep sides it has been dubbed 'Little Switzerland' and 'Yorkshire's Grand Canyon'. There is evidence that both the Romans and Vikings used the gorge system for hiding loot.

'Pillars Past' sculpture encountered along the walk

WALK 7

Pateley Bridge river walk

Start/finish	*Bridge over Nidd, Pateley Bridge*
Locate	*HG3 5HW ///helpless.game.catchers*
Cafes/pubs	*Many cafes, pubs and hotels in Pateley Bridge*
Transport	*Bus 24 from Harrogate and 822 from Ripon/Grassington*
Parking	*At the Showground (exit the car park and turn right to cross bridge to start point). Some free on-street parking and other pay car parks available*
Toilets	*Near the Recreation Ground (south end of bridge over the Nidd) and near Southlands car park (south of the High Street)*

This route explores two different faces of the river and town. The out-and-back walk goes towards Glasshouses and incorporates a sculpture and some industrial history, while the circular walk heads in the opposite direction, offering peace and quiet along the wooded riverside. The tracks are well maintained and level, but Pateley Bridge is a popular destination so can get very busy. When you have finished the walk take time to wander around this picturesque town.

Time 1hr 30min
Distance 5km (3 miles)
Climb 60m

A mellow walk in two different directions along the River Nidd, offering local art, architecture and industrial history

View of the iron bridge to Castlestead

Looking along the River Nidd from Pateley Bridge

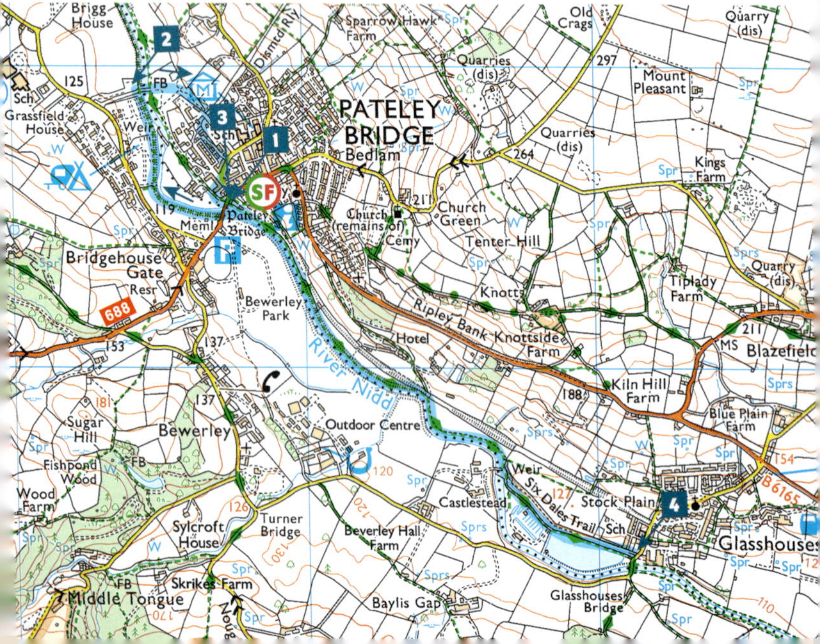

1 The walk can be done in either direction but is described here circular walk first. Start at the north end of the bridge over the **River Nidd**. Cross the bridge and at the end take a right turn to follow an elevated tarmac path that passes the public toilets and playpark. Continue along the path past a holiday park to reach a footbridge.

2 Turn right to cross the footbridge and continue ahead through the woods. The path enters a clearing and passes a BMX track to the left. Follow the path as it enters some more woodland and leaves the public park (Millennium Green). Join a road (Greenwood Avenue) and at the T-junction turn right to follow the road as it curves around to the left to join the High Street and return to the bridge over the River Nidd.

Signpost seen from start

3 From the bridge either take the riverside path or Nidd Walk to follow the signs to the 'Pillars Past' sculptures. Continue past the sculptures, along the riverbank, as the path wends its way through farmland for about 1km to reach a **weir** and an old iron bridge becomes visible. Continue along the path through a gap in a wall and beyond. The large house faintly visible across the river is Castlestead. The path continues, now slightly away from the river, and then charts a course between a pond and small stream.

'Pillars Past', created by Joe Hayton, consists of three life-like sandstone figures of Pateley Bridge's past. The 2m high sculptures are of a miner, a farmer and a monk representing the great pillars of past industries of Nidderdale. They are arranged in a circle and from a distance look like standing stones.

4 Eventually the path reaches **Glasshouses** at a road with a large mill opposite. Turn around and retrace your steps to the start.

Historic building in Pateley Bridge

– To shorten

Omit the loop and simply follow the out-and-back route to Glasshouses for a walk of 3.5km (50min).

Glasshouses and Castlestead

The walk to Glasshouses ends at an old mill that is now residential housing. Between the 1820s and 1900 the mill was owned by the Metcalf family, who lived in Castlestead, the large house visible on the walk. The iron bridge was built to enable easy movement between the house and mill. The mill produced cotton and then flax and hemp rope – it is claimed that rope from Glasshouses was supplied to the *Titanic*. The mill was built in the mid 1700s and closed in early 2000s.

WALK 8

Coldstones Cut

Time 30min
Distance 1.5km (1 mile)
Climb 65m

Contemporary and historic industry and a spectacular piece of artwork with breathtaking views

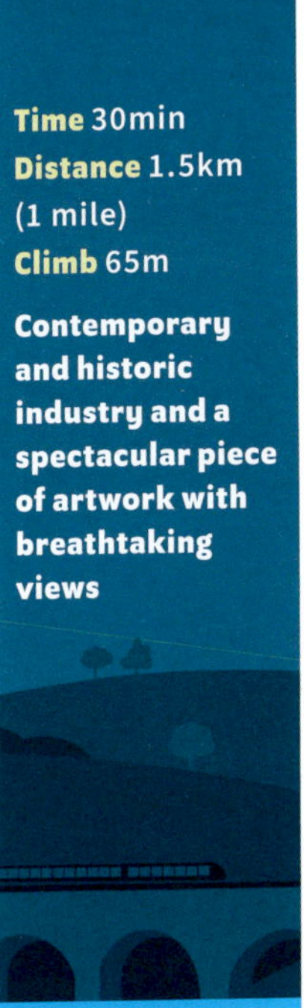

Start/finish	*Toft Gate Lime Kiln near Greenhow*
Locate	*HG3 5BJ \\\velocity.proudest.voted*
Cafes/pubs	*Nothing on route*
Transport	*Bus 822 to start (limited service from Grassington/Pateley Bridge)*
Parking	*Car park at Toft Gate (free)*
Toilets	*No public toilets on route*

This short walk offers a glimpse of local industrial history and current industry alongside an incredible piece of artwork that incorporates great views across Nidderdale and North Yorkshire on a clear day. The paths are well established and clear to follow, but note that this route is located over 1400ft above sea level and therefore can be exposed to sudden changes in weather.

View across Nidderdale from the top of the sculpture

Stone marker post pointing the way

1 Leave the car park by the path to the rear and after 50m come to a stone post.

2 At the post turn left signed to Toft Gates Kiln, go through the gate and follow the path as it descends to the kiln. At the lowest point of the path there are good views of the kiln complex and some supporting information boards. Once you have finished retrace your steps to the fork in the path. At the fork turn left and follow the path gently uphill to reach a single-track road.

3 Follow the path across the road and go through further gates to ascend the clear, wide path to the Coldstones Cut sculpture. This scuplture is Yorkshire's biggest and highest public artwork.

Created by artist Andrew Sabin as a cultural response to the Coldstones Quarry, the Coldstones Cut is public art on a monumental scale. From various platforms visitors can view both the vast limestone quarry below and sweeping panoramas across the Nidderdale AONB (http://thecoldstonescut.org/).

4 At the sculpture walk through the stone corridor to the red 'roundabout', and continue past it to the rear of the complex for views over the vast, operating quarry of Coldstones. At 425m (1400ft) above sea level, Coldstones is one of the highest quarries in Britain and provides over 600,000 tonnes of aggregate a year. Return to the roundabout and turn to either side

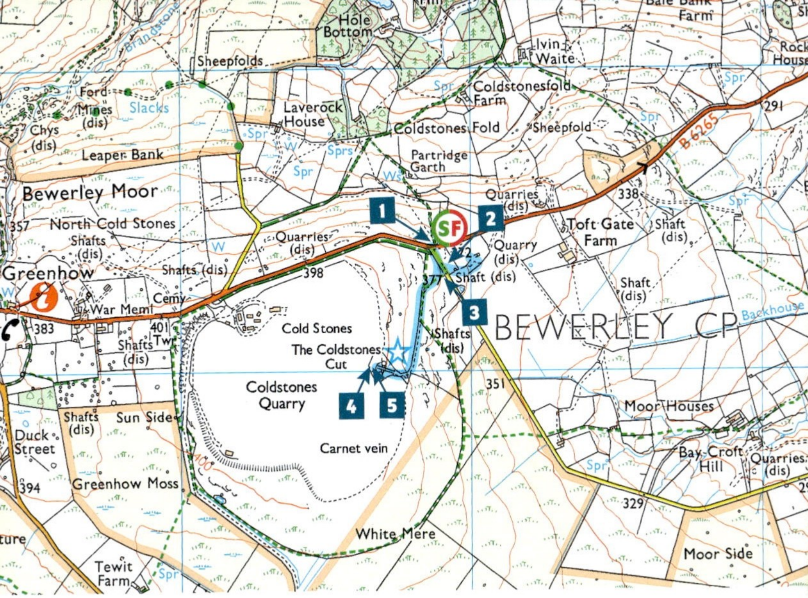

Looking past a limekiln chimney towards Nidderdale

Inside the Coldstones Cut sculpture

to walk to the top of the spiral to take in the great views over the Nidd valley.

In clear weather the North York Moors and Howardian Hills are visible. Closer views could include the 'golf balls' of Menwith Hill, the turbines on Nabbs ridge and the Harrogate skyline.

5 Once you have had your fill of the views simply retrace your steps downhill to the car park.

Looking down into Coldstones Quarry

Strange rock formation at Brimham

WALK 9

Brimham Rocks

Start/finish	*Brimham Rocks*
Locate	*HG3 4DW ///vesting.tourist.slides*
Cafes/pubs	*Cafe at top end of Brimham Rocks*
Transport	*Bus 825 from York/Harrogate/Masham/ Leyburn/Richmond*
Parking	*National Trust car park (free to members) or in laybys 500m north of car park entrance*
Toilets	*Near National Trust cafe*

Time 1hr 20min
Distance 4km (2½ miles)
Climb 140m

An exciting walk which crosses woods, moors and farmland before sampling the dramatic formations of Brimham Rocks

This walk offers everything about the Nidderdale AONB in miniature. In the space of a few kilometres the walk covers woodland, moors and farmland, with fabulous views north and west over Nidderdale and south over Harrogate. It finishes at the spectacular Brimham Rocks with its weird and wonderful rock formations. The walk is well signposted. Allow extra time at the end if you want to explore more of the sculpted rocks.

View east across Brimham Rocks

1 Start at the entrance board by the green metal gates just below the main car park. This is at a junction of the car park road and a gravel track. Follow the gravel track towards Druid's Cave Farm, ignoring the 'Private' sign because a few metres further on can be seen a reassuring yellow footpath sign. Follow the track as it descends past the farm and go through two sets of green metal gates. Continue along the path and through a further green metal gate, and a few metres further on reach some black gates of a house.

2 Stop just short of the black gates and take a footpath off to the left into the woods. Go through a gate and at the track junction turn right to follow the path, with the house to your right. Go through a gap in a wall and follow the path to reach a T-junction, turn left to follow the track down to a footbridge and a ford.

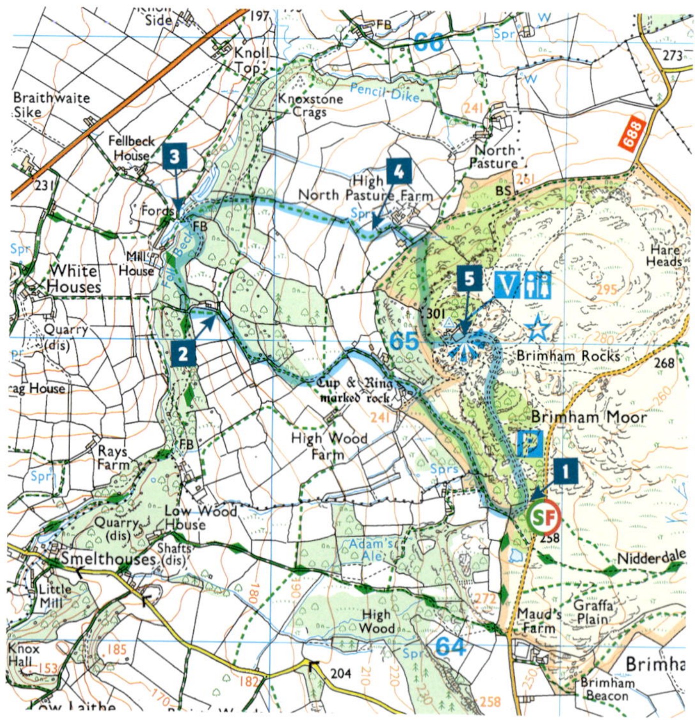

Looking north-east towards the moors of upper Nidderdale

ⓘ Brimham is a Site of Special Scientific Interest (SSSI). The area is home to a variety of wildlife, such as solitary mining bees and the green tiger beetle, as well as various bird species, including meadow pipits, red grouse and finches.

3 Do not cross the bridge but turn right to go through a small metal gate and follow the track as it climbs through a series of fields, eventually reaching another metal gate. Go through this gate, then over a ladder stile. Cross the field to the top left corner to exit over a stile.

4 Follow the track ahead and as you approach the house look right to see a yellow footpath and signs to Brimham. Follow this path across the field and at the far side turn left onto a farm track to exit the farm. A stile to the right leads into National Trust heathland. Cross the stile, then follow the red arrow and take the track at 45 degrees into the woods. This track passes a large rock (Druid's Writing Desk) and joins a larger path. Continue to follow the red signs to the cafe/toilets. Pause here to enjoy the vista of the rock formations, such as the Eagle, in the foreground and Nidderdale in the background.

5 From the cafe follow the 'scenic path' back to the car park. This tarmac path meanders between more fantastic formations such as Castle and Cannon rocks. At the first junction turn right. The start point is just beyond the car park.

Some of the rock formations at Brimham

– To shorten

Skip the walk and just wander around the rocks.

+ To lengthen

From the cafe follow the purple arrows across the moorland to visit the most remote rock formation, the Mushroom. This is an out-and-back walk and adds about 1.5km. The arrow posts are few and far between.

Brimham Rocks

Brimham Rocks are made of gritstone, a fluvial sedimentary rock which was formed by ancient rivers. When glaciers gouged out the Nidderdale valley, the millstone grit was left exposed as the soft rocks were cut away by the ice, leaving these fabulous stacks and rock formations scattered over 50 acres of moorland, now owned by the National Trust. The sculpted rocks have some great names, such as the Sphinx, the Watchdog, the Camel, the Turtle and the Dancing Bear. Brimham Rocks and its heather moorland are both SSSIs and attract geologists, naturalists, climbers and walkers (www.nationaltrust.org.uk/visit/yorkshire/brimham-rocks).

WALK 10

Studley Royal

Start/finish	*Studley Royal National Trust visitor centre*
Locate	*HG4 3DY ///undertook.satin.statement*
Cafes/pubs	*Cafe in visitor centre and one near The Lake*
Transport	*Bus 822 from Ripon/York or Pateley Bridge/Grassington*
Parking	*At visitor centre (free)*
Toilets	*At visitor centre*

Take a tranquil walk through the parklands of Studley Estate, which surrounds Fountains Abbey. There is plenty to delight in this man-made landscape, including herds of deer and sculpted features such as ponds, follies and bridges. The route is well signposted and, if the weather is clear, views of Ripon Cathedral are possible at various points. Note that Fountains Abbey itself is not part of this walk – you will need to pay an entrance fee at the visitor centre to visit the abbey and grounds.

Time 2hr
Distance 6.5km (4 miles)
Climb 120m

A peaceful walk around beautiful parklands and through a secluded valley

Entrance to Studley Royal Deer Park

1 Stand facing the roundabout in front of the visitor centre, cross the road into the car park and follow the path ahead signed for Studley Royal Water Garden. Follow this path as it runs parallel to the exit road (Abbey Road) – there is a screen of trees between the path and road – to reach a side road and white wooden gates off to the right.

2 With a church and obelisk visible ahead, go through the white gate into Studley **Deer Park** and follow the single-track road as it descends to reach a junction. Views open out across the deer park and towards Ripon Cathedral in the distance.

The magnificent St Mary's Church is one of the finest examples of High Victorian Gothic Revival architecture in England. It was designed in the 1870s by the flamboyant architect William Burges.

3 At the road junction turn right down the road to a lake, with another car park and cafe beyond. At the bottom of the slope, as the road bends right, turn left to follow the tarmac path as it skirts the edge of the water. Cross the wide bridge then turn left to follow the path across the first of the 'seven bridges', a series of narrow bridges with fords that cross the meandering River Skell. Follow the path across the bridges through this steep-sided valley to reach a metal fence and gate at the far end, leading into the now abandoned **Chinese Wood**.

ⓘ Fountains Abbey and Studley Royal have UNESCO World Heritage status as a landscape of exceptional merit and beauty, a harmonious whole of buildings, gardens and landscapes. This represents over 800 years of human ambition, design and achievement.

St Mary's Church

Views towards Ripon Cathedral

4 Go through the gate and follow the track, ascending to leave the wood through a gate into farmland. There are views off to the right towards Ripon and the North York Moors. The track descends, passing **Plumpton Hall**. Eventually reach a yellow gatehouse and the main gates to the Studley Estate.

5 Turn left through the arch and walk along the road through the Deer Park as it climbs back to Waypoint 3, then retrace your steps to the start.

Looking across the lake to the 'fishing tabernacle'

– To shorten

Follow the route to Waypoint 3, then walk to the far end of the lake and cafe and back to the start. This gives a walk of 4km (1hr 20min).

+ To lengthen

At Waypoint 5, once inside Studley Deer Park, turn right and follow the boundary wall until you reach the obelisk and church at Waypoint 2, then return to the visitor centre. This adds about 2km (40min) to the walk.

Studley Royal Estate and Deer Park

One of the seven bridges across the Skell river

John Aislabie inherited the Studley Royal Estate in 1693. An ambitious man, he became Chancellor of the Exchequer but in 1720 was expelled from Parliament due to his part in the South Sea Bubble financial scandal. He returned to Yorkshire and devoted himself to creating this ground-breaking garden. The 850-acre Deer Park is home to over 500 wild red, fallow and sika deer and is a World Heritage Site. The seven bridges are an extension of the pleasure gardens and trace the Skell River valley. The walk is thought to have been first laid out in 1742 and was designed to provide a picturesque approach to the Chinese Gardens at the eastern end (www.nationaltrust.org.uk/fountains-abbey-and-studley-royal-water-garden).

Stepping stones on the River Nidd

WALK 11

Dacre Banks riverside walk

Start/finish	*Dacre Banks*
Locate	*HG3 4EN (pub opposite car park) ///edits.chiefs.perky*
Cafes/pubs	*Pub at the start, cafe in Darley*
Transport	*Bus 24 runs between Harrogate and Pateley Bridge*
Parking	*Small car park in Dacre Banks (free)*
Toilets	*Public toilets near green in Dacre Banks*

A pleasant, well-signposted walk between two picturesque villages that offers views and history in abundance. The walk meanders through farmland along the River Nidd and gives glimpses of a long-lost industrial past by following an old railway line for some of the way. Old railway features can be seen at most points on the walk, as well as great views along this part of the Nidd valley.

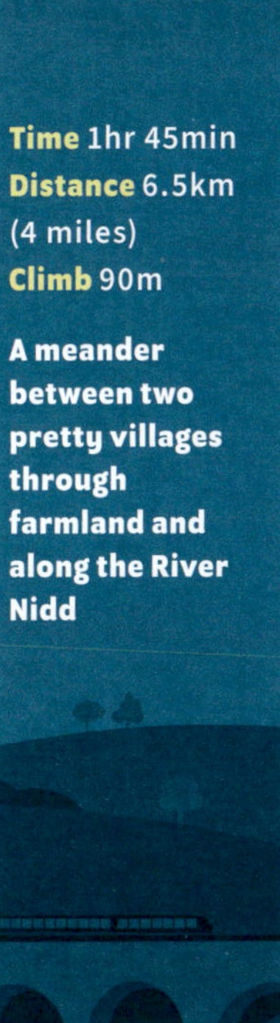

Time 1hr 45min
Distance 6.5km (4 miles)
Climb 90m

A meander between two pretty villages through farmland and along the River Nidd

Looking back towards Dacre Banks

Summerbridge
Dacre Banks
Dacre
Darley
Darley Head
Nidderdale Way
River Nidd
Low Hall
Low Hall Wood
Dover Castle
Pyefield House
Stocks Green
Stepping Stones
Clough House Farm
Dowgill Farm
Dougill Hall
Manor House Farm
Manor House Wood
Throstle Nest
White Oak
Hartwith
Hartwith Hill
Birch Hill
Eastwoods Farm
Hill Top Farm
High Beren House
Dacre Hall
Beeston Farm
Mill Hirst
Mill Hirst Farm
Clocken Syke Farm
Broker Crags
Low Hirst
Darley Bridge
Rushfield Farm
Oxen Close
The Carr
Carr Farm
Ivy House Farm
Crake House Farm
Pine Tree Farm
Holly Tree Farm
Hardgroves Hill
Menwith Hill Farm
Sheepcote Hill
Fringill
Low Green
Moke Hill Farm
Walker Lane
Darley Carr
Whin Bush Farm
West Wood
Ell Knowle Wood
Horse Coppice
Old Spring Wood
Standing Stone Hill
Willie's Wood
Dismtd Rly
B 6451
B 6165
1
2
3
4
5

1 Turn right out of the car park to follow a gravel track. After about 100m follow the footpath as it trends slightly right, with a wall to your right. Go through a gap in the wall and cross the field ahead, aiming for the top corner, then through a metal gate to join the old railway track. Go through a further two gates then follow the footpath straight ahead into a field. Leave the field through a red farm gate onto a road at **Low Hall**.

The Nidd Valley Railway was an 18.5km single-track branch railway line that ran along the valley of the River Nidd. It ran from Ripley Junction, on the Harrogate to Ripon Line, to Pateley Bridge stopping at Ripley Valley, Hampsthwaite, Birstwith, Darley, and Dacre.

2 Cross the road and continue straight ahead through the farmyard. Go through a metal gate to exit the farmyard and enter **Low Hall Wood**. Reach another farm gate to enter a field, cross the field to a small gate, turn right and follow the path uphill through a gate, then turn left to follow a broken wall. Reach a further gate and cross a concrete road. Continue ahead through a further gate into a field and to a stile, cross the stile then go through a wooden gate into a small wood. Follow the path downhill to a farm gate into a field on your right, then exit the field through a gap in the wall into a further field to reach a ford/bridge. All is well signposted with yellow-and-white footpath signs.

3 Cross the bridge and follow the path uphill to the pretty village of

Footbridge at Waypoint 3

Stocks at Stock Green

Stocks Green. Pass between some houses to reach the road, keeping a look out for some stocks and information boards, and turn left to follow the road towards Darley. After 200m turn left onto Station Road and go downhill to the river. Refreshments are available at a cafe further along Station Road.

4 When you reach the river turn left, signed 'Footpath River Nidd'. Cross a footbridge and follow the clear path along the **River Nidd**, noting various bits of railway architecture and the stepping stones in the river on the way. The path leaves the riverbank at one point to continue along the edge of a field for about 30m. In the field ignore a stile and continue beyond to a kissing gate to get back to the river, following yellow footpath signs.

> ⓘ ***The train station for Dacre was closer to Summerbridge than Dacre and so the settlement nearer the train station was called Dacre Banks.***

5 Stay with the riverbank as the houses of **Dacre Banks** become visible. When you reach a gate in a wire fence turn left to cross a field leading to a track, then turn left and almost immediately right onto a small road to return to the start.

– To shorten

After Waypoint 2 where the path turns right at the end of the first field after the woods, turn left instead, down to the river, and follow the path back to the start, saving 30min.

+ To lengthen

After Waypoint 3 rather than turning left onto Station Road, continue along the road to Nidd Lane, turn left and when you meet the river turn left again to rejoin the route. Adds about 2km (40min) to the walk.

Old railway bridge viewed from the river bank

Entrance gate to Ripley Castle

WALK 12

Ripley circular

Time 1hr 15min
Distance 4.5km (2¾ miles)
Climb 100m

A short wander through a picturesque village and around an historic estate offering plenty of views and history

Start/finish	*Ripley*
Locate	*HG3 3AX (village) ///marmalade.skewed.found*
Cafes/pubs	*Pub, cafe and shops in Ripley*
Transport	*Bus 36 from Ripon, Harrogate and Leeds*
Parking	*Pay car park at the south end of Ripley village, plus limited free on-street parking*
Toilets	*In car park at start*

This short walk delivers views across the lower Nidd and some interesting history along the way. It starts and ends in the picturesque estate village of Ripley that is home to a 14th-century church and Ripley Castle, one of the finest historic houses in England, then goes through the Ripley Estate, giving an insight into local history and the Nidd valley. The way is well signposted and mostly on good tracks. In spring the bluebells in the woods are amazing.

Ripley Castle seen from the route

Follow the castle walls towards the bridge over the River Nidd

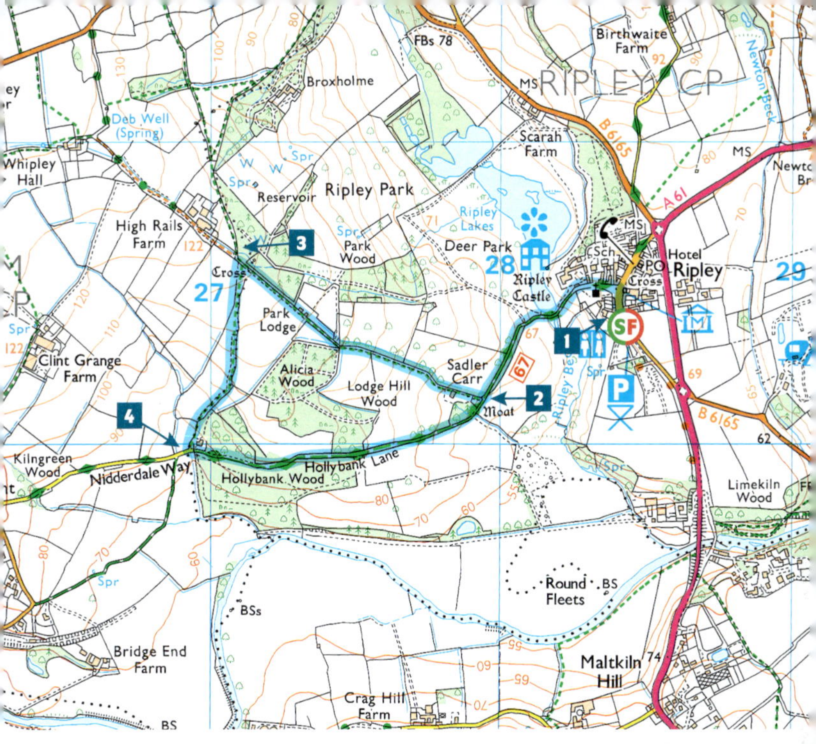

1 From the car park walk into the village and turn left to walk between the church and the entrance to **Ripley Castle**. Follow the track as it crosses then ascends beyond the river. After a few hundred metres the bridleway arrives at a junction at **Sadler Carr**.

> ⓘ *Henry Ingilby of Ripley Castle collected taxes for Edward III (1312–1377) and helped the King to finance the construction of Windsor Castle.*

2 Turn right to follow the track as it passes a barn to the left. Follow the track as it ascends to a ridge, then the gradient eases as you pass **Park Lodge**. Approximately 250m after Park Lodge a hedge can be seen running at a tangent to the path on the left – on the other side is a gate and a sign-posted footpath into a field.

3 Go through the gate and down through the field keeping the fence on the left. As the path descends enjoy the views across the Nidd valley towards Harrogate. At the bottom of the field go through a gate in the corner and continue to descend, now between hedges. The path quickly reaches a tarmac track.

4 Turn left and take the wooden gate onto bridleway 67 (this is the second gate visible), which follows **Hollybank Lane** to the track junction at Sadler Carr. Then retrace your outward route past the castle and back to the village.

– To shorten

At Waypoint 2 do not turn right but walk straight on to Waypoint 4 and return (approximately 2km or 40min).

Ripley church and signpost

Looking along the entrance to the castle grounds

Ripley Castle

A Grade 1 listed building, Ripley Castle is over 700 years old and has been owned by the Ingilby family for all that time. The family crest is a boar's head, which is displayed in many places around the castle. Nine of the 11 conspirators of the 1605 Gunpowder Plot were relatives of the family, and James I (VI of Scotland) stayed at the castle on his way to his coronation in 1603. The gardens and grounds include a deer park, lakes, hothouses and a kitchen garden, and are open daily 10am–2pm. There are seasonal guided tours to the castle (www.ripleycastle.co.uk).

The emblem of the Ingilby family is a boar

River Nidd and railway bridge in Knaresborough

WALK 13

Nidd Gorge

Start/finish	*North end of the A59 bridge, Knaresborough*
Locate	*HG5 9AX ///crackles.mass.crumple*
Cafes/pubs	*Plenty of pubs, cafes, tea rooms and shops in Knaresborough, pub at Old Bilton on route*
Transport	*Trains and buses to Knaresborough*
Parking	*Pay car park by the bridge. Some free on-street parking nearby*
Toilets	*Knaresborough and Old Bilton*

Time 2hr 30min
Distance 9km (5½ miles)
Climb 175m

A pleasant walk through woods and along the River Nidd that starts and ends in picturesque Knaresborough

Solitude, nature and views abound on this walk through farmland and woods. Starting and ending in the picturesque town of Knaresborough, the walk follows the River Nidd and rises through farmland, giving views across the Dales and occasional glimpses of the skylines of Harrogate and Knaresborough. It is well signposted but it can be muddy underfoot in places.

Signposts along the route

Monument to cycling legend Beryl Burton

1 Head south across the bridge and turn immediately right at the end of the bridge to take the riverside path (signposted '636 cycleway'). Follow this path through a park with the **River Nidd** to your right, passing a monument to Beryl Burton.

Beryl Burton was a Leeds-born cycling legend who dominated women's cycling throughout the 1950s and 60s. This walk follows

a short distance on the cycleway dedicated in her memory. Take time to read of her incredible achievements.

2 Approximately 50m beyond the monument there is a path junction. Follow the tarmac path uphill to your left, signposted to Starbeck. Pass a picnic area and at a signpost for Bilton/Starbeck go through a gate with a small cattle-grid. Follow the path as it ascends across farmland to reach a road junction.

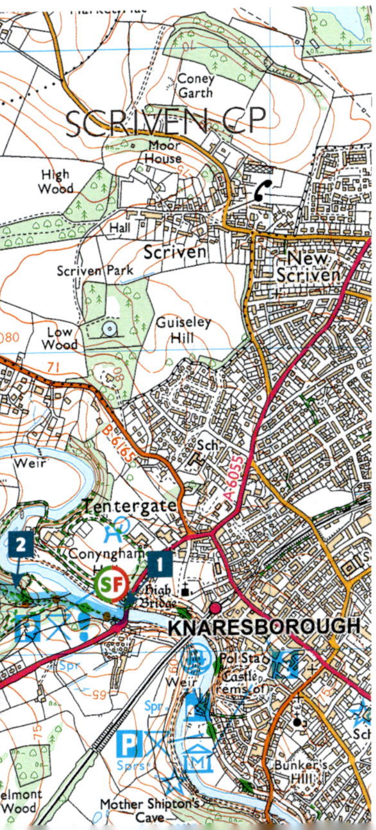

The name Knaresborough describes its original defensive site on the top of craggy cliffs: 'knarre' meaning rocky outcrop in Anglo-Saxon, and 'burgh' meaning fortress.

3 At the road junction (with Bilton Hall to the right) continue straight ahead along a single-track road, Bilton Lane (signposted 'Ringway footpath/636 cycleway'). The road passes a campsite to the right and descends to a pub (Gardiner Arms) at **Old Bilton**.

4 As you pass the pub look out for a signed footpath immediately off to the right. Take this path as it descends to cross a stream and then climb to the right of Woodside Farm. There are good views off to the Dales at this point. Enter a narrow gap between hedges and drop down into woods onto a wooden walkway until the river comes into view.

5 At a signpost turn right to follow signs to Nidd Gorge. After about 50m this path descends to the riverside and the gorge itself, which runs the length of the river section of this walk. Follow the river until it crosses a fence (signpost to Nidd Gorge). The path then

Looking across to Knaresborough on the return route

ascends and reaches a footbridge across the river.

The Nidd Gorge is a steep-sided valley and includes wetlands, ancient woodland and new native woodland. This variety of habitats supports a plethora of wildlife, so you may see meandering deer or kingfishers working the river.

6 Continue past the bridge without crossing it and follow the sign for Knaresborough. The path climbs away from the river on a wooden walkway to reach the top of the slope. Take a sharp left turn along the edge of the woods. Cross a stile and meet the single-track road, Bilton Lane, once more. Turn left to retrace your steps to Knaresborough.

– To shorten

On the outbound leg turn right about 200m beyond the road junction after Waypoint 3/ Bilton Hall to take the path to the river. Follow the river to the bridge at Waypoint 6 and return (approximately 6km, 2hr).

Looking along the Nidd Gorge

Sunset over Swinsty Reservoir

WALK 14

Swinsty Reservoir circular

Time 1hr 30min
Distance 5km (3 miles)
Climb 70m

A relaxing walk through woodland and around the reservoir, offering views and tranquillity

Start/finish	*Swinsty and Fewston Reservoir*
Locate	*LS21 2NP ///suffix.political.purely*
Cafes/pubs	*None on route, pub in Timble (1km away on North Lane)*
Transport	*Bus 821 from Keighley/Otley or Pateley Bridge*
Parking	*Car park at reservoir (free)*
Toilets	*At start*

A pleasant and relaxing walk around a large reservoir, offering views along and across the picturesque Washburn valley. The walk passes through woods and for most of the way keeps close to the edge of the reservoir, presenting different views as it progresses around the water. It can be muddy in places but is well signposted with little climbing. It can be done in either direction but anticlockwise, described here, offers the best views.

The route crosses Swinsty dam

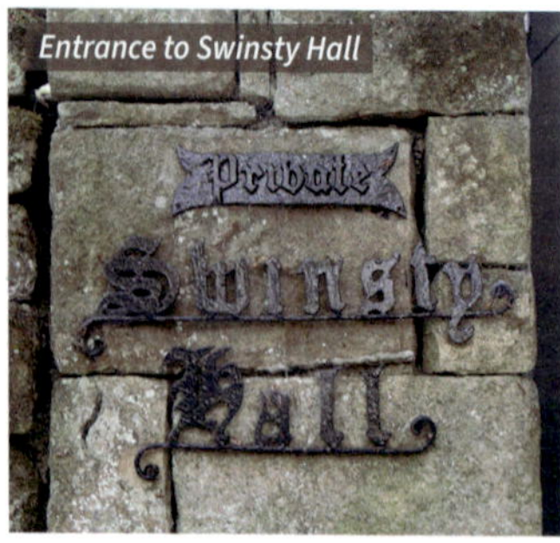

Entrance to Swinsty Hall

1 From the entrance to the car park turn right then right again to follow the footpath that runs behind the toilets. At the track junction continue straight ahead towards a large house (**Swinsty Hall**). Continue along the track as it passes the house, come to a T-junction and turn right to follow the track along the edge of **Swinsty Reservoir**, then at the end of the track turn left to cross the dam (all permissive paths). Construction on Swinsty Reservoir was begun by the Leeds Waterworks Company in 1871 and completed in 1878.

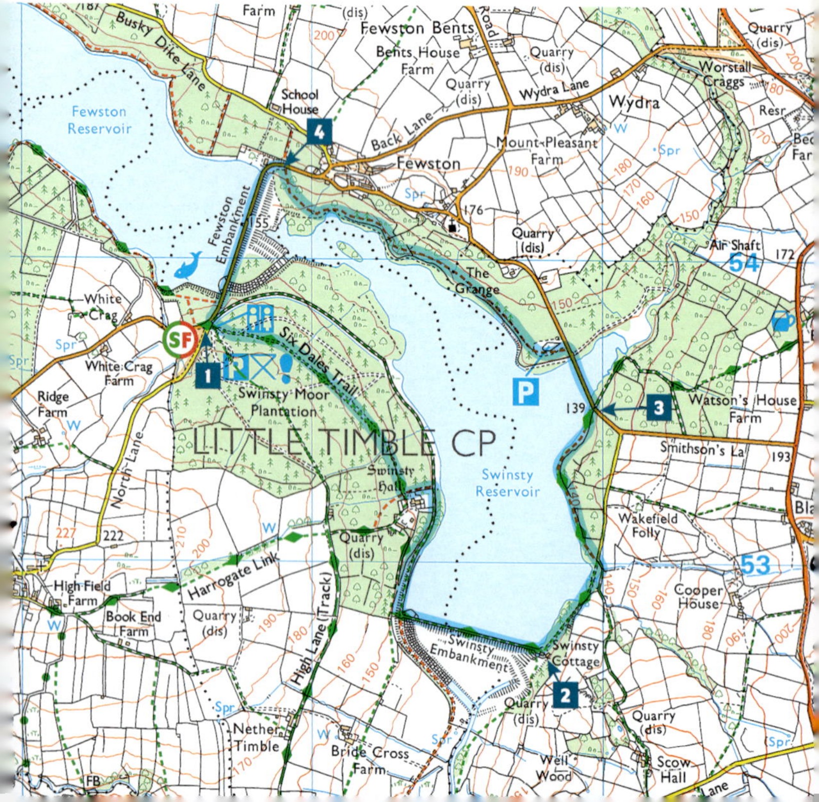

Picnic area by the reservoir

> ⓘ ***Underneath Swinsty Reservoir lie the remains of New Hall. In the 17th century this was the home of Elizabethan poet Edward Fairfax.***

2 At the far end of the dam follow the tarmac road as it bends to the left. Stay with the road to reach some metal gates with footpaths crossing the road. Turn left along the Yorkshire Water permissive path. This path meanders along the side of the reservoir and eventually reaches a road.

3 Turn left onto the road and cross the bridge. (There is no footway on the bridge so care is needed.) The body of water to the right is Swinsty Lagoon, a popular fishing area. At the far end of the bridge turn left off the road and pass through a picnic area with a car park behind trees. The path meanders away from the water and climbs through trees to a gap in a stone wall.

4 Go through the gap to rejoin the road, turn left and cross the dam. The water to the right is Fewston Reservoir. At the far end follow the road back down to the starting point.

– To shorten

On the outbound leg, at the T-junction just beyond Swinsty Hall, rather than turn right, take a left to return directly to the start point (2km, 40min).

View along the Washburn valley

Washburn valley

Four reservoirs have been built in this beautiful valley. Between 1869 and 1966 Lindley Wood, Swinsty, Fewston and Thruscross reservoirs were constructed to cope with the rapid growth of Leeds and Bradford and high demand for water. Visit the heritage centre near Fewston church (signposted from the walk) for more of the history of this once picturesque valley. In 1816 the artist J W Turner toured Yorkshire and produced a number of pictures as a result. One was a sketch and watercolour called 'On the River Washburn below Folly Hall, Looking to Dob Park Castle'. The picture is in the Tate Gallery in London for all to see.

Old packhorse road through trees

WALK 15

Washburn valley circular

Start/finish	*Lindley Bridge at south end of Lindley Wood Reservoir*
Locate	*LS21 2QN ///muscular.newsreel.remote*
Cafes/pubs	*None on route*
Transport	*No public transport*
Parking	*Small car parks either side of Lindley Bridge (free)*
Toilets	*No public toilets on route*

Time 3hr
Distance 9.5km (6 miles)
Climb 260m

An extensive walk by water, through woods and across farmland showcases the wonderful Washburn valley

This walk is one of two halves. The first is a gentle walk around the reservoir and along the river, the second is a climb along an old packhorse road to a high point. The effort is rewarded with great views over the Wharf valley, Almscliffe Crag and towards Harrogate. The reservoir itself remains quite elusive on this walk with limited views and glimpses through trees. Parts of the walk are muddy but it is well signposted and easy to follow.

Dam at the eastern end of Lindley Wood Reservoir

1 Start at the north end of the bridge. An old, faded signpost 'Footpath Norwood Bottom' directs you along a path that crosses the left-hand side of a private drive to a house, into woodland. Follow the path as it skirts **Lindley Wood Reservoir**, with occasional glimpses of the water along the way. At the far end turn left onto a road and cross the bridge. (There is no footway on the bridge so care is needed.)

2 Immediately across the bridge go into the layby then follow the footpath sign to exit through the rear over some stone steps by a gate. Continue along the path until it turns right to cross a bridge. Cross over a stile on the far side then turn left to follow the **River Washburn**. The path curves towards a gate that leads into woods, then reaches another gate. At this point look left for a stile onto the track.

3 Turn left onto the track and cross the small bridge, **Dobpark Bridge**, next to the ford. The ford is thought to date from medieval times, while the unusually narrow bridge was built in the 17th century for packhorses. Once over the bridge follow the Six Dales Trail along the cobbled track

Dobpark packhorse bridge

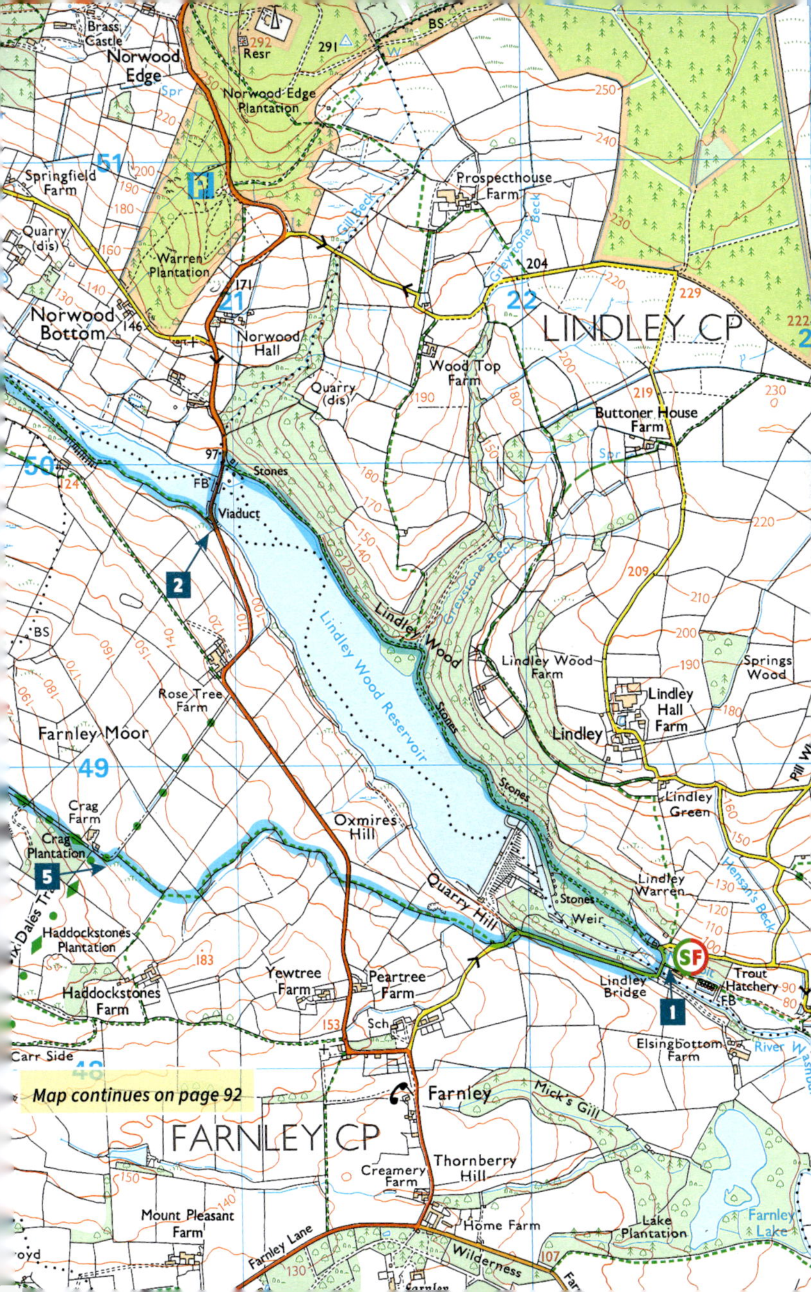

Map continues on page 92

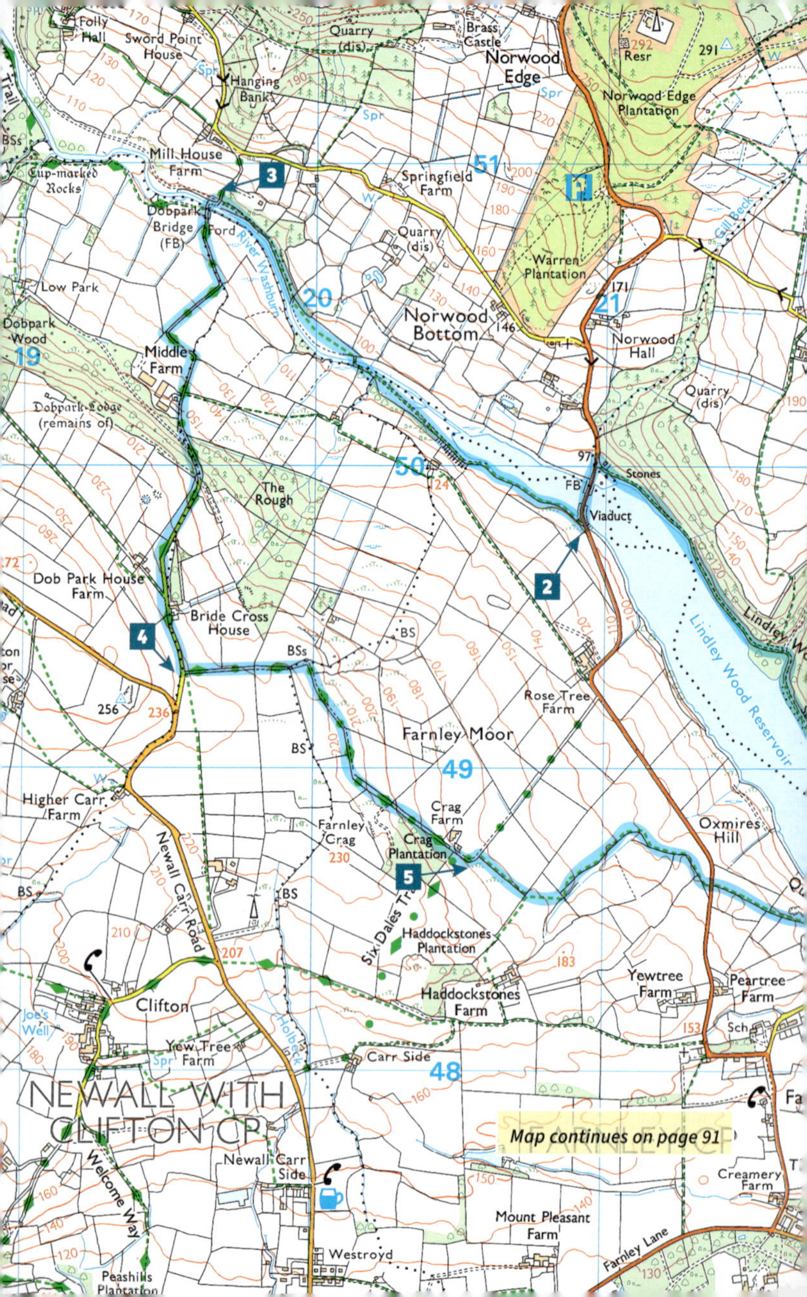
Folly Hall
Sword Point House
Hanging Bank
Quarry (dis)
Brass Castle
Norwood Edge
Resr
292
291
Norwood Edge Plantation
Mill House Farm
3
Springfield Farm
51
Cup-marked Rocks
Dobpark Bridge (FB)
Ford
River Washburn
Quarry (dis)
Warren Plantation
Gill Beck
Low Park
20
Norwood Bottom
146
171
21
Norwood Hall
Dobpark Wood
19
Middle Farm
Quarry (dis)
Dobpark Lodge (remains of)
The Rough
50
124
97
Stones
FB
Viaduct
2
Dob Park House Farm
Bride Cross House
BS
BSs
4
256
236
Rose Tree Farm
Lindley Wood Reservoir
Farnley Moor
49
BS
Higher Carr Farm
Farnley Crag
230
Crag Farm
Crag Plantation
Oxmires Hill
5
Newall Carr Road
BS
BS
Six Dales Trail
Haddockstones Plantation
183
207
210
Clifton
Haddockstones Farm
Yewtree Farm
Peartree Farm
Joe's Well
Yew Tree Farm
Holbeck
Carr Side
153
Sch
48
NEWALL WITH CLIFTON CP
FARNLEY CP
Map continues on page 91
Newall Carr Side
Welcome Way
Creamery Farm
Mount Pleasant Farm
Westroyd
Farnley Lane
Peashills Plantation

Signs for the Six Dales Trail

> ⓘ ***Packhorse bridges, like Dobpark Bridge, were often built on trade routes to allow goods to be transported between towns and villages, before the development of turnpike roads and canals.***

straight ahead. The track heads uphill, passing Middle Farm, and eventually turns into a tarmac road. Continue to follow the road uphill as it passes some houses and the entrance to **Dob Park House Farm**. The gradient starts to ease and a telecoms mast is visible ahead. At this point look out for a footpath post with three choices.

4 Follow the signs for the Six Dales Trail to the left. Take time to enjoy the views across the Washburn valley towards Almscliffe and Harrogate, while off to the right the Wharf valley can be seen. The track descends through a gate, then bends to the right and a farmhouse becomes visible. Go down past **Crag Farm** to join a tarmac track.

View across the valley to Almscliffe Crag

5 As the track bends sharp left go through the farm gate to the right with a footpath sign. Cross the field and go through a further gate. Once on the other side turn left to climb a ladder stile into a further field. Follow a faint path down through the field, keeping a wire fence to the right. The path bends right, parallel to a road, to reach some steps over the stone wall. Once over the steps cross the road at a slight diagonal to reach a footpath on the other side. Go through the stile to cross the field and through a further gate, with the dam now visible. Cross a further field to a further gate onto a single-track road. Turn left and follow the road downhill back to the start.

– To shorten

Walk as far as the bridge across the reservoir at Waypoint 2 and return the same way, giving a walk of about 5km (1hr).

Almscliffe Crag

Almscliffe Crag, visible on this walk, will be recognised by fans of the television series *Emmerdale*. The crag was used in the opening credits from 1998 to 2005 and can occasionally be seen in wide-angle shots of the Yorkshire countryside in scenes set in the garden of Hawthorn Cottage and Home Farm.

USEFUL INFORMATION

Tourism bodies

Nidderdale AONB
https://nidderdaleaonb.org.uk

Nidderdale
www.nidderdale.co.uk

Transport

Dales Bus timetable
www.dalesbus.org/timetable.html

Trainline for rail times and tickets
www.thetrainline.com

Tourist information

Knaresborough: Castle Courtyard, Knaresborough, HG5 8AE
visitharrogate.co.uk

Masham: Little Market Place, Masham, HG4 4DY
visitmasham.com

Otley: Nelson Street, Otley, LS21 1EZ
visitotley.co.uk

Pateley Bridge: Station Square, King Street, Pateley Bridge, HG3 5AT
tel 01423 714953

Ripon: Market Place, Ripon HG4 1DD
visitharrogate.co.uk

Weather

Met Office
www.metoffice.gov.uk/weather/forecast/uk

Mountain Weather Information Service
www.mwis.org.uk

First edition 2023
ISBN: 978 1 78631 154 2

Printed in China on responsibly sourced paper on behalf of Latitude Press Ltd
A catalogue record for this book is available from the British Library.

CICERONE

Cicerone Press, Juniper House,
Murley Moss, Oxenholme Road,
Kendal, Cumbria, LA9 7RL

www.cicerone.co.uk

Updates to this Guide

While every effort is made to ensure the accuracy of guidebooks as they go to print, changes can occur during the lifetime of an edition. Any updates that we know of for this guide will be on the Cicerone website (www.cicerone.co.uk/1154/updates), so please check before planning your trip. We also advise that you check information about transport, accommodation and shops locally. We are always grateful for updates, sent by email to updates@cicerone.co.uk or by post to Cicerone, Juniper House, Murley Moss, Oxenholme Road, Kendal, LA9 7RL.

Register your book: To sign up to receive free updates, special offers and GPX files where available, register your book at www.cicerone.co.uk.